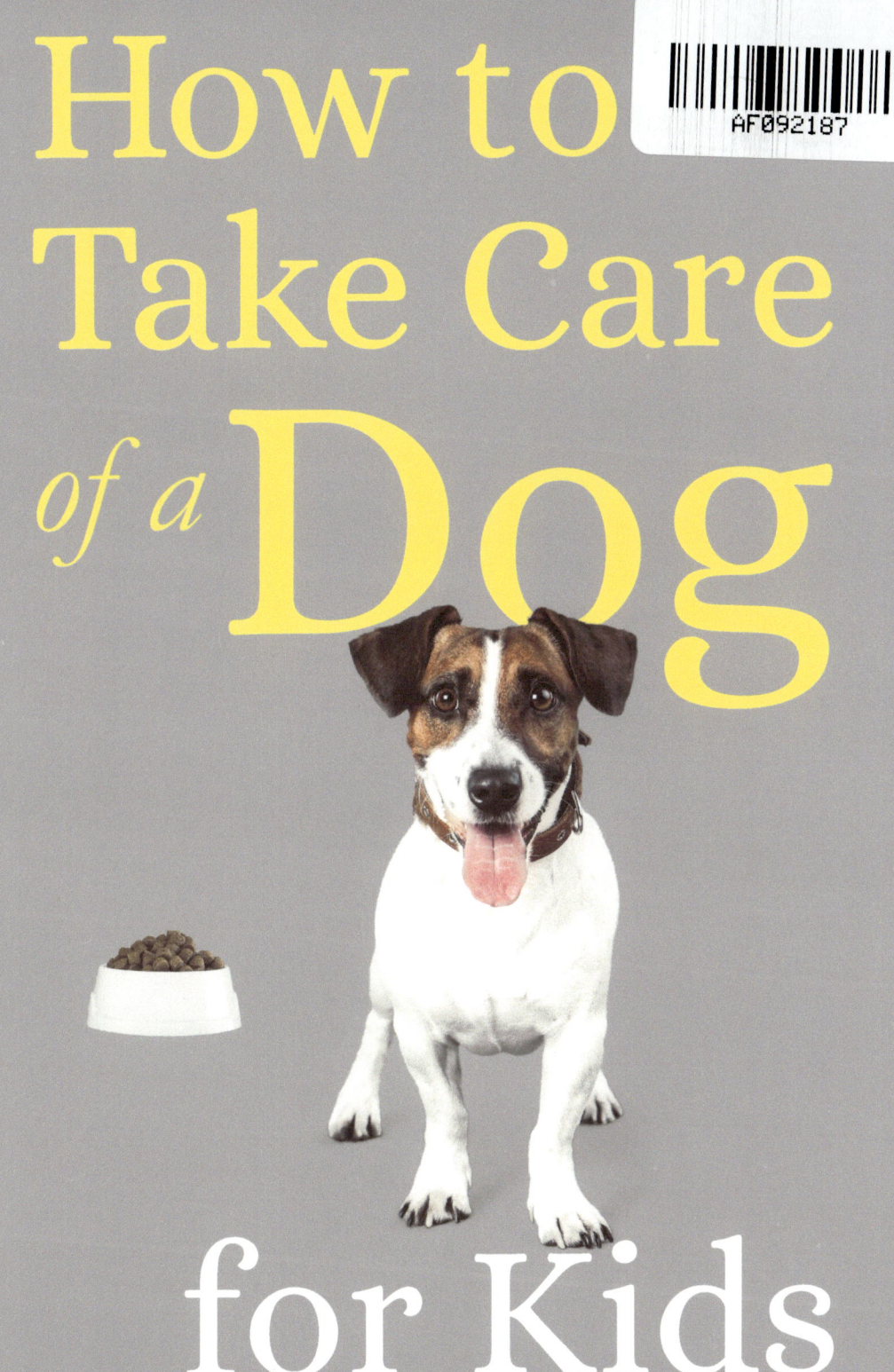

How to Take Care of a Dog for Kids

How to Take Care of a Dog for Kids
© 2025 All Rights Reserved.
No part of this publication may be reproduced, distributed, or transmitted in any form or by any means, without the prior written permission of the copyright holder.

TABLE OF
CONTENTS

Introduction	*Page 4*
Chapter 1 Getting Ready for a Dog	*Page 7*
Chapter 2 The First Day Home	*Page 11*
Chapter 3 Feeding Your Dog	*Page 16*
Chapter 4 Health and Grooming	*Page 19*
Chapter 5 Exercise and Playtime	*Page 23*
Chapter 6 Learning Basic Commands	*Page 28*
Chapter 7 Solving Common Problems	*Page 31*
Chapter 8 Responsibility and Love	*Page 36*
Conclusion	*Page 39*

Introduction

Welcome to **How to Take Care of a Dog for Kids!**

If you are holding this book, you are likely excited about becoming a dog owner or already have a wonderful furry friend in your life. This guide is your complete handbook dedicated entirely to the essential task of learning how to take care of a dog for kids.

Owning a dog means taking on a big, important job that comes with incredible rewards. Dogs rely completely on us for their happiness and health, and this book will teach you exactly how to meet their needs every single day.

What to Expect from This Book

This guide is structured to walk you step-by-step through the journey of dog ownership:

• **Part I: Bringing Your New Friend Home** focuses on preparation. We will discuss how to choose the right dog for your family, what supplies you absolutely need before they arrive, and the best way to handle The First Day Home so your new pet feels safe and calm.

• **Part II: Daily Dog Care and Routines** covers the everyday essentials. You will learn about proper nutrition, including Feeding Your Dog and understanding treats, as well as the important routines of Health and Grooming. We also dive into how much Exercise and Playtime your dog needs to stay healthy and happy.

- **Part III: Manners and Training** teaches you how to communicate with your dog. You will discover tips for using positive rewards to teach Learning Basic Commands like "sit" and "stay," and how to manage and resolve common issues like house-training accidents or jumping as we cover Solving Common Problems.

- **Part IV: Being the Best Dog Owner** brings it all together, emphasizing the vital importance of Responsibility and Love in building an unbreakable bond with your pet.

By the time you finish this book, you will have the confidence and knowledge necessary to ensure your dog lives a joyful, healthy life, proving you are a truly caring and responsible canine companion!

Part I: Bringing Your New Friend Home

Chapter 1: Getting Ready for a Dog

Bringing a new dog into your life is incredibly exciting! Proper preparation is essential to ensure your new furry friend has the best possible start. Preparing adequately before bringing a dog into your home sets the foundation for a positive pet ownership experience.

Choosing the Right Dog for Your Family

Before your pup comes home, the first step is selecting a dog that will be a harmonious match with your family's lifestyle and home environment.

Considering Size and Breed

It is crucial to consider factors like size and breed. Understanding the specific needs of different breeds is essential. Different dog breeds vary in size and characteristics.

- **Size and Space:** Larger breeds may require more space and exercise, while smaller breeds are often better suited for apartment living. Researching various breeds can help you find one that fits well with your home environment.

Energy Levels and Temperament

Each dog has its own energy levels and temperament. Matching the dog's energy level to your family's activity level is essential for a happy coexistence.

- Some dogs are **highly active** and require plenty of exercise.
- Others are more laid-back and enjoy lounging around.

Dog-Proofing the House and Yard

Ensuring your home is safe for your dog is a necessary part of the preparation process. Dog-proofing involves securing hazardous items out of reach. By making your home safe, you can help prevent your dog from finding and swallowing harmful objects.

Supplies Checklist

Before bringing your new companion home, you must have all the necessary supplies ready to provide a comfortable living environment for your dog.

Food and Water Essentials

Dogs need to eat regularly and should have access to food. They also need plenty of **clean water** daily.

- **Bowls:** Invest in **durable stainless steel bowls** for food and water. Stainless steel bowls are long-lasting, safe for pets, easy to clean, and help maintain hygiene.

Walking Gear

A reliable leash is vital for walks and outings with your dog.

- **Leash and Harness:** Before you head out on your first walk, make sure your dog has a **well-fitting harness** and a **good sturdy leash**. You can opt for a **double-handle leash** made of **sturdy nylon material** for added control during walks.

- **ID Tags:** Don't forget to attach an **ID tag** with your contact information in case your dog ever gets lost.

Resting and Comfort

Your dog needs a cozy space to rest.

- **Dog Beds**: A dog bed is needed so your dog can rest properly. You can create a cozy space by investing in an elevated bed that provides comfort and support.

- **Crates:** If you use a dog crate, responsible owners must ensure the crate is large enough for the dog to stand up and turn around comfortably. The crate should allow room for his food and water bowl. The crate should have a solid floor free of debris and dust, and should include a dog bed where your dog can rest properly.

Toys and Play

Providing toys helps keep your dog entertained and stimulates their mind.

- **Selection:** Choose toys that are strong enough to withstand play and won't break apart into small pieces that your dog could swallow or choke on.

- **Interactive Toys**: Interactive toys, such as Kong toys, stimulate your dog's mind and help prevent boredom.

- **Training Tools:** Controlling access to the toys, and not letting them have them at all times, can help increase the power of that toy as a training tool. If a dog plays with the same toy every day, he might get bored.

Clean-Up Supplies

You must pick up after your dog when they go to the bathroom. Dogs usually prefer to potty outside.

- **Poop Bags:** Bring poop bags! Picking up your dog's waste is a big favor to your neighbors.

Chapter 2: The First Day Home

The first day your dog arrives is a big moment! This chapter will help you handle the first few hours calmly and establish a safe routine for your new companion, which is essential for learning **how to take care of a dog for kids.**

How to Introduce the Dog to the House Calmly

When introducing a new pet, it is important to take things slow and let your new dog settle in without rushing the process.

Building Trust Through Interaction

Always make sure that the dog actually wants to be petted, even if the dog is your own. You should never push your dog too hard.

1. **Approach Slowly**: Let the dog come to you first.
2. **Allow Sniffing:** When the dog approaches, let him smell your hand so he knows he can trust you before you dive in. If you do not do this, the pup could become mad or anxious.
3. **Petting Techniques:** For basic petting, stroking a dog "head-to-tail on the back is best". Until you know the animal very well, it is best to avoid the mouth, paws, and belly. Be aware that some dogs may not enjoy having certain spots touched, such as the head, belly, tail, or ears. Always start a petting session with a gentle stroke down the back before trying out other methods.
4. **Finding the Sweet Spot:** Once you both warm up to each other, you can try to find the dog's "sweet spot," or his favorite place to be pet, which is sometimes on his belly or right above the base of his tail.
5. **Reading Body Language**: Children need to become "detectives and decode the animal's body language". Watch the animal's body and ask: Does its body feel tense? Is the dog giving you the side eye?. If the answer is yes, these are messages that the animal needs a break.

Important Safety Rules:

- Never pet a dog if he eats or has food in his mouth.
- Do not touch a dog's head or tail.
- Do not tease a dog or play aggressively with him; if a child does this, she may get bitten.

Meeting Other Family Members and Pets Safely

Supervising children during interactions with dogs ensures safety for both the child and the pet.

Introducing the Dog to Children
If you have young children, it is important to take things slow when introducing the new pet.
- **Take the Lead:** Let the children take the lead in getting to know the dog, and do not push them too hard. If they are not interested in interacting, that is okay; let them come around at their own pace.
- **Positive Interactions:** Introduce your dog to your child in a positive way, such as allowing the child to stroke the dog.
- **Supervision and Boundaries: Do not allow your children any time alone with the dog**. Always set physical boundaries between your dog and child, especially if they are not introduced properly.

- **Toddler Safety:** If the children are babies or toddlers, keep them aside for at least an hour after your dog's bedtime to prevent the dog from attacking a child left alone with him.
- **Leash Use:** If you are unsure about allowing children to interact with your pet, consider using a leash. You must keep a close eye on your dog while they are interacting.

Creating a Safe Den or Resting Spot

Your dog needs a place to retreat where they can rest properly. Crate training is a good idea, especially if you plan to leave your dog alone for long periods.

Crate Guidelines

- **Size:** Responsible dog owners must ensure that the crate is large enough for the dog to stand up and turn around comfortably. If the crate is too small, your dog could injure himself or become claustrophobic.
- **Movement:** Your dog should have enough room to turn around in his crate while eating or sleeping.
- **Comfort:** The crate should have a firm, clean floor, free of debris and dust.
- **Bedding:** The crate should include a dog bed where your dog can rest properly.
- **Supplies:** The crate should allow room for food and water bowls.

If you think your dog might be anxious in a crate, you can take them out and do some basic exercises beforehand, such as walking around the house or playing tug of war.

Part II: Daily Dog Care and Routines

Chapter 3: Feeding Your Dog

Providing the right nutrition is essential for your dog's health and well-being. Feeding your new dog properly is important not only for their health but also helps to build a positive bond with you.

Choosing and Providing the Right Food

The food you choose should be appropriate for your dog's life cycle —whether they are a puppy, an adult, or an older dog—as their nutritional needs change throughout their lives.

Choosing High-Quality Food

It is best to feed your dog a high-quality diet specifically made for dogs. When selecting dog food, look for options that are rich in nutrients and contain ingredients like real meat, vegetables, and whole grains to keep your dog energized. The diet should include plenty of protein, carbohydrates, and healthy fats.

Getting Advice

There are so many different types of dog food available that it can be overwhelming, so the advice of your **veterinarian** can help you sort through the possible choices. It is important to consult with your veterinarian about the best type of food for your dog.

Establishing a Feeding Schedule

Maintaining a consistent feeding routine helps regulate your dog's digestion and prevents overeating. You should set specific meal times each day to create a sense of structure for your pet.

How Often to Feed

Your veterinarian can also help you figure out how much and how often to feed your dog to make sure they stay healthy.

- **Puppies** should be fed several times a day as they can burn through their energy quickly.
- **Older dogs** generally do well being fed twice a day.

Monitoring Food Amount

It is best to feed your dog according to the feeding chart on the bag of food. It is important to feed them plenty to be in good physical condition, but **excessive food is extremely harmful** to them. Extra weight can lead to problems with their joints and bone structure, as well as with their internal organs.

You will know you are giving the right amount of food when your pet is in **lean and athletic condition**, with no bones showing along their back and rib cage, but also no excessive weight hiding the shape of their muscles.

Eating Etiquette

When you feed your dog, make sure you are using **clean food bowls** and that you are leaving them to eat in peace. Some dogs can get aggressive if they think their food is about to be stolen from them.

Understanding Treats and Safe Hand Feeding

Giving treats and food by hand can be a great way to bond and train your dog, but it must be done safely to prevent dangerous nipping or snatching.

Giving Treats Safely

To safely give hand-delivered food to your pet, place a nugget of dry food or a treat in your **closed hand** and offer it at nose level to the dog. **Only open your hand when the dog is polite** and not trying too aggressively to get the food out. This method ensures they don't become nippy and try to snatch the food out of your fingers.

It is great fun to see your dog focus as they learn that you are the source of tasty food. If your dog is on the heavier side, using their own dry kibble instead of store-bought treats can cut down on calorie intake.

Table Scraps

If you have a dog used to getting food from the table, it is best to start feeding them in their room where they can be supervised, and ensure they don't get too much food from the table.

Clean Water

A vital part of proper feeding is ensuring your dog has access to hydration. Always keep a **fresh bowl of clean water** available for your dog to drink out of at all times of the day.

Chapter 4: Health and Grooming

Learning how to take care of a dog for kids means keeping your dog clean, comfortable, and healthy. Proper health care and grooming habits are vital for your dog's overall well-being.

Grooming Essentials

Dogs need consistent grooming to stay healthy and look their best. It is important to start grooming your dog at a young age so it becomes a comfortable routine.

Brushing and Bathing

Regular brushing is necessary for all dogs.

- **Brushing Technique:** The proper way to groom a dog is with a brush from head to tail. Start at the base of the neck and work your way down, ensuring you get all the way to the skin. If your dog has long hair, you must also comb it out regularly.

- **Why Brush?** Frequent brushing will help prevent painful mats from forming and will also help reduce excessive hair in the household. Be careful not to scrub too hard or irritate the skin when brushing.

- **Bathing:** If your dog needs a bath, try to make it a stress-free experience. Bathing should be done as needed, using gentle shampoo suitable for dogs and room temperature water.

Nail Trimming

Trimming your dog's nails is essential to prevent overgrowth and discomfort.

- You will need specialized nail clippers to trim your dog's nails.

- Be cautious not to cut too close to the quick (the pink part inside the nail), as this can be painful.

Ear Cleaning

As part of grooming, you will also need to clean your dog's ears. You should clean your dog's ears with a cotton ball and some ear cleaner.

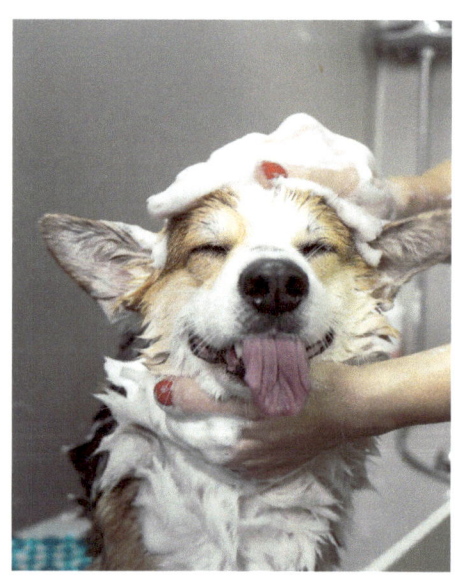

Dental Care

Just like humans, you need to pay attention to your dog's teeth. You can start brushing your dog's teeth with dog-safe toothpaste to make the process fun and easy for both you and him. It is best to do this with a parent's help.

Preventing Pests (Parasite Protection)

Flea and tick prevention is super important to keep both you and your dog safe and healthy.

• **Consult Your Veterinarian**: You should consult with your veterinarian regarding parasites. Your vet will guide you on what is best for your dog to help keep them safe.

• **Monthly Prevention:** After 6 months of age, dogs should get monthly preventatives for heartworm, fleas, and ticks. Fleas and ticks can often be prevented with a large variety of products that are simply applied to the skin once a month.

The Veterinarian and Overall Health

Regularly visiting the vet is crucial for your furry friend's well-being. Check-ups help ensure your dog is healthy and catch any issues early.

Vet Visits

When going to the veterinarian:

• It is important that **the dog needs to be calm and relaxed** (no pulling on the leash, barking, or whining in the waiting room). If your dog is anxious, it will only make the visit more difficult for them.

• Remember that vets are there to help animals, not to scare them. Always remember to thank the vet for their time and care.

• **Vaccinations** play a vital role in preventing diseases that can harm your dog.

Spaying and Neutering

One of the most important things you can do for your dog is to have them spayed (for females) or neutered (for males).

- **Procedure:** These are common surgical procedures performed to prevent dogs from reproducing.

- **Benefits:** The benefits of spaying and neutering far outweigh the risks. This surgery helps control the pet population and provides health benefits. Spayed or neutered pets are less likely to develop certain cancers, and they tend to be less aggressive and more social than unaltered counterparts.

Chapter 5: Exercise and Playtime

Keeping your dog active is key to their overall health and happiness. Dogs require regular activity to stay physically healthy and mentally sharp.

Why Exercise is Important for Your Dog

Exercise is a critical component of proper dog care. Dogs need to play to **stimulate their minds and bodies** just like you do.

- **Health Benefits:** Exercise will help keep your dog healthy and happy. Dogs need at least **30 minutes of exercise per day** to stay healthy. The more activity they get, the more calories they burn, which helps prevent excessive weight.

- **Mental Stimulation:** Regular walks not only provide physical exercise but also offer mental stimulation for your dog. Taking them on different routes helps to keep things exciting and engaging, preventing boredom.

- **Behavior and Calmness:** Allowing dogs to get frisky and playful with games helps them understand the limits of play and when they need to be more calm. Doing basic exercises beforehand, like walking around the house or playing tug of war, can also help an anxious dog feel relaxed.

Different Types of Exercise and Play

There are many fun ways to incorporate exercise into your daily routine and strengthen the bond between you and your pet.

• **Daily Walks:** Regular walks are one of the best ways to provide physical and mental stimulation.

• **Fun Games:** Interactive games are wonderful ways to engage with your pet. Playing games of fetch or tug-of-war stimulates their mind and body. You can also engage in interactive games like hide-and-seek with your furry companion.

• **Yard Time:** Playing fetch in the yard is another great way to exercise your dog.

How to Play with and Walk Your Dog Safely

Playing with your dog should always be a positive and safe experience.

Safe Play with Toys

Toys help keep your dog entertained, but you must choose them carefully.

• **Toy Selection:** Choose toys that are strong enough to withstand play and won't break apart into small pieces that your dog could swallow or choke on.

• **Interactive Toys:** Interactive toys, like Kong toys, stimulate your dog's mind and help prevent boredom.

• **Toy Power:** Controlling access to the toys (and not letting them have them at all times) can help increase the power of that toy as a training tool. If your dog plays with the same toy every day, he might get bored.

• **Never Play Aggressively:** Do not tease a dog or play aggressively with him; if a child does this, she may get bitten.

Walking Responsibly

Before heading out on your first walk, make sure your dog has a well-fitting harness and a good sturdy leash.

• **Adult Supervision:** If you have a big dog, you will want to bring an adult with you to make sure your pup doesn't pull you over.

• **Pulling Correction:** If your dog starts to pull on the leash, stop walking and wait for them to calm down before continuing. This teaches them that pulling gets them nowhere.

• **Picking up Waste:** Always bring poop bags! You need to pick up after your dog when he does his business—it's a big favor to your neighbors.

• **Public Safety:** Keep your dog on a leash when walking in public places.

Part III: Manners and Training

Chapter 6: Learning Basic Commands

Teaching your dog basic commands is a fundamental part of learning how to take care of a dog for kids. These simple cues are essential for communication, safety, and creating a strong foundation for all future training.

Tips for Using Positive Reinforcement

Effective training relies heavily on positive reinforcement techniques. This means rewarding your dog for doing something right, which encourages them to repeat that behavior.

- **Reward Good Behavior:** When your dog follows a command correctly, immediately reward the good behavior with treats or praise.

- **Focus is Fun:** It is great fun to see your dog focus as they learn that you are the source of tasty food, and thus the most interesting thing in their environment.

- **Treat Technique:** To safely give food by hand, place a nugget of dry food or a treat in your closed hand and offer it at nose level. Only open your hand when the dog is polite and not trying aggressively to snatch the food. This technique ensures they don't become nippy and try to snatch food out of your fingers, which can be dangerous.

Teaching the Basics: "Sit," "Stay," and "Come"

Start with simple commands like "Sit," "Stay," and "Come." These three cues are fundamental.

Teaching "Sit"

"Sit" is one of the most basic commands.

- You can teach "Sit" by holding a treat in front of your dog's nose.
- Slowly move the treat upwards until your dog's rear end hits the ground. As soon as the dog sits, give the reward and praise them.

Teaching "Stay"

"Stay" is an important command that can help keep your dog safe, especially when you are not around.

The Importance of Consistency

Even after your dog has learned these basic commands, you must keep enforcing them. If you stop reinforcing the commands, your dog may start reverting to bad habits.

Starting with the Leash

Before learning advanced commands, your dog needs to be comfortable with their equipment. The first step in training is getting your dog comfortable wearing a leash.

1. **Introduce the Leash Calmly:** Start by putting the leash around your dog's neck without attaching it to anything.
2. **Praise and Reward:** Treat your dog and give them lots of praise when they are calm and relaxed while wearing the leash.
3. **Practice Inside:** Once your dog is comfortable with the leash, attach it to their collar and walk them around your home for a few minutes.
4. **Walking Manners:** When walking, if your dog starts to pull on the leash, you must stop walking. Wait for them to calm down before you continue. This teaches them that pulling gets them nowhere and only calm behavior results in forward movement.

Chapter 7: Solving Common Problems

Even the best-behaved dogs can sometimes face challenges. Learning how to handle common problems like accidents inside, pulling on the leash, or unwanted begging is an important part of learning **how to take care of a dog for kids.**

House-Training and Accidents

House training is one of the most common challenges new dog owners face. Consistency is key to teaching your dog where they should potty.

Establishing Consistency

It is important to **start house training immediately** when you bring your new dog home. You need to be consistent with your commands and routines. Dogs usually prefer to potty outside, which is generally the easiest solution.

Cleaning Up Accidents

If accidents happen inside the house, it is important to **clean them up** right away. If you don't clean thoroughly, the dog might get used to going potty in the house because they can still smell where they went before.

Stopping Unwanted Behaviors

Sometimes dogs develop behaviors that are annoying or potentially dangerous, such as pulling on the leash or snatching food. Learning how to gently correct these behaviors is essential.

Enforcing Obedience and Preventing Bad Habits

Obedience training helps prevent bad habits. Once your dog has learned basic commands like "sit," "stay," and "come," you must keep enforcing these commands. If you stop reinforcing them, your dog may start reverting to bad habits.

Leash Pulling

If your dog starts to pull on the leash while walking, you must stop walking. Wait for them to calm down before continuing to move forward. This teaches them that pulling gets them nowhere, and only calm behavior allows the walk to continue.

Nipping and Snatching Food

To prevent nipping or snatching food, you must teach your dog to be polite when taking food from your hand.

- **Treat Technique:** Place a nugget of dry food or a treat in your closed hand and offer it to the dog at nose level.
- **Polite Behavior:** Only open your hand when the dog is polite and not trying aggressively to snatch the food.
- This method is important because it ensures your dog does not become nippy and try to snatch food out of your fingers, which can be very dangerous.

Aggression and Boundaries

When feeding your dog, make sure you are leaving them to eat in peace. Some dogs can get aggressive if they think their food is about to be stolen from them.

If you are concerned about your dog's behavior:
- If the dog barks or growls, you should stop what you are doing and back away slowly.
- Do not tease a dog or play aggressively with him; if a child does this, she may get bitten.
- Do not try to handle an aggressive dog yourself; if the dog is being aggressive, call the police.

The Importance of Socializing Your Dog

Socialization helps your dog grow up to be confident and comfortable in the world.

Meeting Other Animals

Allow your dog to meet different dogs in a controlled environment. This helps them learn social skills and build confidence around other animals. However, you should generally avoid hanging out with your dog where there are other dogs, especially in uncontrolled settings, unless you know they are safe.

Interacting with People

Encourage interactions with various people, including family members, friends, and strangers. This exposure helps your dog become comfortable in different social settings.

Doggy Daycare

If you regularly take your dog on walks or are away during the day, you can take your dog to a doggy daycare. This will allow your dog to run around, play with other dogs, and socialize. The more time spent outside, the better.

Handling Table Scraps

If you have a dog used to getting food from the table, it is best to start feeding them in their room where they can be supervised. If your dog gets food from the table, it's important to ensure they don't get too much, as excessive weight is harmful to their health.

Part IV: Being the Best Dog Owner

Chapter 8: Responsibility and Love

You have learned all the essential information on how to take care of a dog for kids—from training and feeding to health and grooming. This final chapter celebrates the incredible commitment and love that comes with being a responsible dog owner.

The Commitment Required to Own a Dog

Caring for a dog is one of the most fun and rewarding experiences you can have! It is also a valuable lesson in responsibility and compassion for children. Owning a dog offers a remarkable opportunity to teach important life skills like empathy, respect, and self-regulation.

Your commitment means ensuring your dog has their basic needs met every day: regular meals, clean water, exercise, and good hygiene. By actively involving yourself in tasks like feeding, walking, and grooming, you are nurturing your dog's well-being and instilling valuable life skills, including commitment and accountability.

Setting clear rules and responsibilities helps you understand your important role in caring for your dog. Remember, consistency is key!

How to Build a Strong, Loving Bond

The journey of caring for a dog involves more than just providing food and water; it is about instilling values like empathy, responsibility, and respect.

To build an unbreakable bond with your pet:

1. **Become an Expert:** You should do everything in your power to become the world's top expert on your dog. Learn about their nutritious foods and how you can best train them.
2. **Spend Quality Time:** Spend good, quality time bonding with your dog through play and activity. Playing games, such as fetch or tug-of-war, stimulates their mind and body and strengthens your friendship.
3. **Positive Support:** Encouraging your dog and giving them positive support fosters confidence and ensures a happy life.

The unconditional love and companionship dogs offer create lasting memories. By taking on the commitment of dog care, you will have a best friend for life!

Safety Rules for Interacting with Your Pet

Even when you are best friends, safety must always come first. Prioritizing safety is crucial to ensure a harmonious relationship between you and your pet.

- **Decode Body Language:** Remember to be a "detective and decode the animal's body language." Watch your dog's body and ask: Does its body feel tense? Is the dog giving you the side eye? These signals mean your animal needs a break.
- **Safe Petting:** Always let your dog come to you first. Start any petting session with a gentle stroke down the back and avoid the mouth, paws, and belly until you know the dog very well.
- **Boundaries:** Never pet a dog if he eats or has food in his mouth, and do not tease or play aggressively with him. Professional trainers suggest that setting clear rules and physical boundaries ensures a harmonious relationship.
- **In Public:** Always keep your dog on a leash when walking in public places to ensure safety for everyone.

By remembering the importance of responsibility, safety, and love, you and your furry friend can enjoy a long and happy life together. Embrace the joy of having a dog as part of your family!

Conclusion

In conclusion, you have successfully learned the essentials of how to take care of a dog for kids. Caring for a dog is truly a fun and rewarding experience that goes far beyond just completing a task. It is a valuable lesson in responsibility and compassion for children.

By following all the tips and guidelines in this book, you have gained the knowledge necessary to ensure your pet's well-being, including proper feeding, walking, and grooming. This experience has helped instill valuable life skills such as empathy, respect, and self-regulation.

Now that you have the basics down, you are ready to be the best friend possible to your new canine companion. You should do everything in your power to become the world's top expert on your dog. Continue to learn about nutritious foods, effective training methods, and remember to spend good, quality time bonding with your dog.

Embrace the joy of having a dog as part of your family. The unconditional love and companionship they offer create lasting memories, and you will have a best friend for life.

By following these tips and continuing to show commitment, you and your furry friend can enjoy a long and happy life together.

www.ingramcontent.com/pod-product-compliance
Lightning Source LLC
LaVergne TN
LVHW070438080526
838202LV00038B/2841